HAL•LEONARD
INSTRUMENTAL PLAY-ALONG

AUDIO
ACCESS
INCLUDED

FLUTE

MANNHEIM STEAMROLLER
Christmas

T0070903

To access audio visit:
www.halleonard.com/mylibrary

Enter Code
3674-9931-3338-3243

Audio Arrangements by Peter Deneff

ISBN 978-1-4803-9705-7

HAL•LEONARD®
CORPORATION
7777 W. BLUEMOUND RD. P.O. BOX 13819 MILWAUKEE, WI 53213

In Australia Contact:
Hal Leonard Australia Pty. Ltd.
4 Lentara Court
Cheltenham, Victoria, 3192 Australia
Email: ausadmin@halleonard.com.au

Visit Hal Leonard Online at
www.halleonard.com

CONTENTS

BRING A TORCH, JEANETTE ISABELLA

FLUTE

17th Century French Provencal Carol
Arranged by CHIP DAVIS

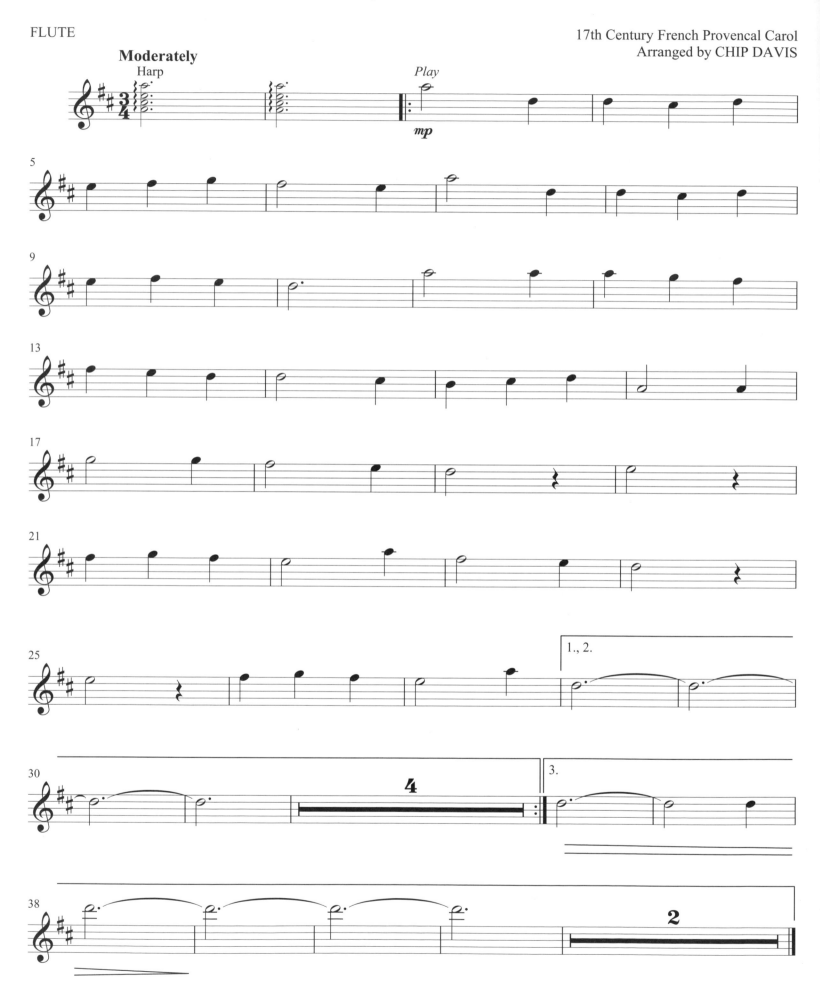

GOOD KING WENCESLAS

FLUTE

Arranged by CHIP DAVIS

CAROL OF THE BELLS

Ukrainian Christmas Carol
Arranged by CHIP DAVIS

FLUTE

7

CHRISTMAS LULLABY

FLUTE

By CHIP DAVIS

DECK THE HALLS

FLUTE

Arranged by CHIP DAVIS

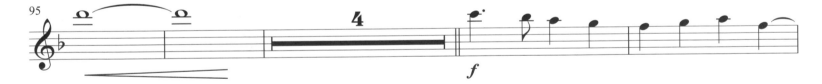

GOD REST YE MERRY GENTLEMEN

FLUTE

19th Century English Carol
Arranged by CHIP DAVIS

GREENSLEEVES

FLUTE

Sixteenth Century Traditional English
Arranged by CHIP DAVIS

Play 8va if desired

HARK! THE HERALD ANGELS SING

FLUTE

By FELIX MENDELSSOHN
Arranged by CHIP DAVIS

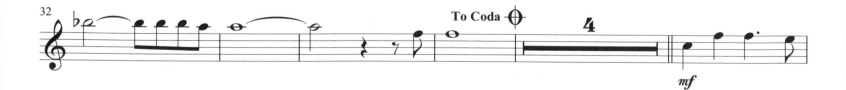

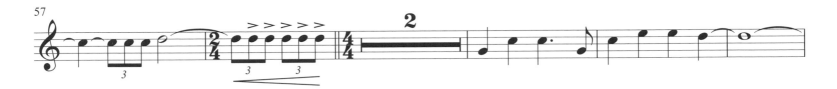

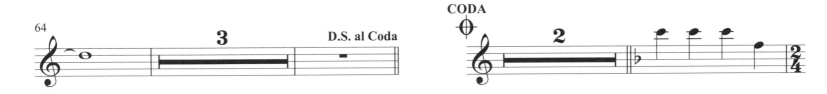

JOY TO THE WORLD

FLUTE

Arranged by CHIP DAVIS

PAT A PAN

Flute

Words and Music by BERNARD DE LA MONNOYE
Arranged by CHIP DAVIS

SILENT NIGHT

FLUTE

Arranged by CHIP DAVIS

TRADITIONS OF CHRISTMAS

FLUTE

By CHIP DAVIS